A Note to Parents

DK READERS is a compelling programme for beginning readers, designed in conjunction with leading literacy experts, including Maureen Fernandes, B.Ed (Hons). Maureen has spent many years teaching literacy, both in the classroom and as a consultant in schools.

Beautiful illustrations and superb full-colour photographs combine with engaging, easy-to-read stories to offer a fresh approach to each subject in the series. Each DK READER is guaranteed to capture a child's interest while developing his or her reading skills, general knowledge and love of reading.

The five levels of DK READERS are aimed at different reading abilities, enabling you to choose the books that are exactly right for your child:

Pre-level 1: Learning to read
Level 1: Beginning to read
Level 2: Beginning to read alone
Level 3: Reading alone
Level 4: Proficient readers

The "normal" age at which a child begins to read can be anywhere from three to eight years old. Adult participation through the lower levels is very helpful for providing encouragement, discussing storylines and sounding out unfamiliar words.

No matter which level you select, you can be sure that you are helping your child learn to read, then read to learn!

Penguin Random House

For Dorling Kindersley
Editor Vicki Taylor
Designer Jill Clark
Senior Slipcase Designer Mark Penfound
Senior DTP Designer Kavita Varma
Producer David Appleyard
Managing Editor Sadie Smith
Managing Art Editor Ron Stobbart
Creative Manager Sarah Harland
Art Director Lisa Lanzarini
Publisher Julie Ferris
Publishing Director Simon Beecroft

Reading Consultant Maureen Fernandes

For Lucasfilm
Executive Editor J. W. Rinzler
Art Director Troy Alders
Keeper of the Holocron Leland Chee
Director of Publishing Carol Roeder

This edition published in 2015
First published in Great Britain in 2010 by
Dorling Kindersley Limited,
80 Strand, London, WC2R 0RL

This edition produced for The Book People,
Hall Wood Avenue, Haydock, St. Helens WA11 9UL

Slipcase UI: 001–291320–Oct/15

Page design copyright © 2015 Dorling Kindersley Limited.
A Penguin Random House Company

A CIP catalogue record for this book
is available from the British Library

ISBN: 978-1-4053-5099-0

Printed in China.

www.starwars.com
www.dk.com

A WORLD OF IDEAS:
SEE ALL THERE IS TO KNOW

DK READERS

BEGINNING TO READ ALONE

2

STAR WARS

Join the Rebels

Written by Catherine Saunders

My name is Luke Skywalker.
I live on Tatooine with my
Uncle Owen and Aunt Beru.

My uncle wants me to be a farmer but I would prefer to go to the Imperial Academy.

I want to be a pilot like my friend Biggs Darklighter.

C-3PO and R2-D2
Uncle Owen bought these droids from Jawa traders. C-3PO is a protocol droid. He can speak many languages.
R2-D2 is an astromech droid.

My life is very quiet on Tatooine.

It is a remote desert planet.

Every day, I help my uncle on

his moisture farm.

But I dream of adventure!

Life is much more exciting in other parts of the galaxy. It is also more dangerous. An evil Emperor rules the galaxy. He has built a powerful weapon that can destroy a whole planet. It is called the Death Star.

Some brave people have joined
together to try and defeat the
Emperor. They are called the Rebel
Alliance. I would like to join them.
The Emperor wants to destroy the
Rebels but he does not know where
to find them.

The Rebels have a secret base on Yavin 4. This is where they plan secret attacks on the Empire.

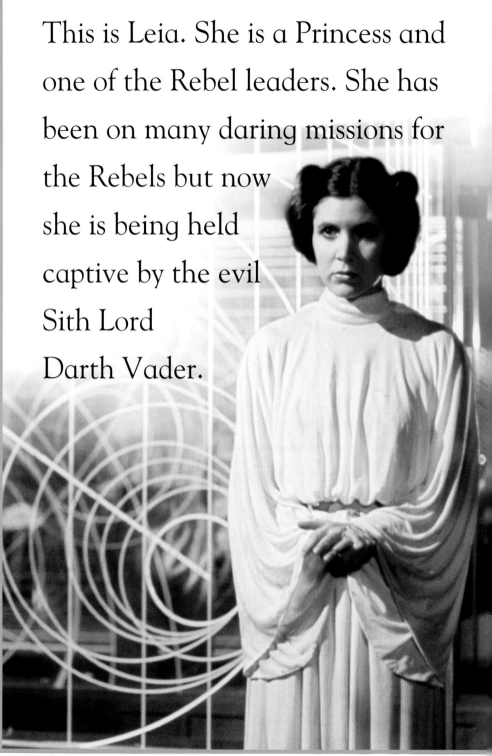

This is Leia. She is a Princess and one of the Rebel leaders. She has been on many daring missions for the Rebels but now she is being held captive by the evil Sith Lord Darth Vader.

My uncle's new droid R2-D2 has
a message from Princess Leia.
She needs help from Jedi Master
Obi-Wan Kenobi.
I am going to help, too!

Darth Vader

Darth Vader was once
a famous Jedi but now
he serves the Emperor.
He wants to crush the
Rebel Alliance.

Princess Leia has hidden the blueprints of the Death Star inside R2-D2. Obi-Wan and I must take them to Princess Leia's home planet, Alderaan. We need to go there quickly! The *Millennium Falcon* will fly us there. It is one of the fastest ships in the galaxy.

Han Solo is its captain and a Wookiee named Chewbacca is his first mate.

The planet Alderaan has been destroyed by the Death Star! Now we are caught in a tractor beam and are being pulled toward the Death Star.

I am a long way from Tatooine
and heading straight into a
thrilling adventure.

I am determined to rescue Princess
Leia and join the Rebel Alliance.

Being a Rebel hero is not easy.
The Imperial stormtroopers are
firing at us from all directions.
Now we are trapped in a smelly
garbage dump.

After many adventures, we escape
from the Death Star and rejoin
the Rebel Alliance. I am ready to
help the Rebels fight back against
the evil Empire.

Rebel pilots must be ready for action at all times. We are on a mission to destroy the Death Star. It is very dangerous but I am learning to use the Force.

The Force

The energy that surrounds all living things. Jedi knights use the power of the Force. Sith lords use the dark side of the force for evil.

I am flying a ship called an X-wing and the Imperial pilots are attacking us in TIE fighters. Many of my brave Rebel friends have already been lost. Luckily I have scored a direct hit and the Death Star is destroyed.

My first mission was a success.
The Rebels were triumphant
and everyone was so happy.
I felt like a hero.
Now I am learning that being a
Rebel is hard work. Imperial spies
are everywhere and we must
always be on the look out
for them.

The new Rebel base on Hoth is very cold.

The Imperial forces have
discovered our new base!
The stormtroopers have giant
AT-AT walkers and are trying to
destroy our power source.

The Rebels are ready for action and are not going to give up without a fight. I have a plan… This battle is over and the Rebels must flee from Hoth. We will live to fight another day.

The Battle of Hoth was a victory for the Empire but the Rebels are not beaten yet. We will overcome the Empire and free the galaxy. I am going to Dagobah to meet the famous Yoda and learn the ways of the Force. I will become a great Jedi warrior.

Yoda
Yoda may be small but he is a very powerful and wise Jedi. He senses that Luke has great powers and shows him how to use them.

The Force is showing me that
my good friends Han Solo and
Princess Leia are in danger.

Darth Vader has set a trap for
them in Cloud City.

I need to rescue them.

I was right. Darth Vader is here.

I must fight him and help free
my friends.

The Rebel Alliance is growing stronger. There is a new Death Star. We have a plan to destroy it and finally defeat the Empire.

Moon of Endor

Endor's forest moon is home to creatures called Ewoks. They may look cute but they are tough! The Ewoks help the Rebels to destroy the new Death Star.

The Death Star's shield generator is located on the moon of Endor. The Rebels are going to attack it!

The plan is working.

The shield generator is destroyed and the Rebel pilots are attacking the Imperial fleet.

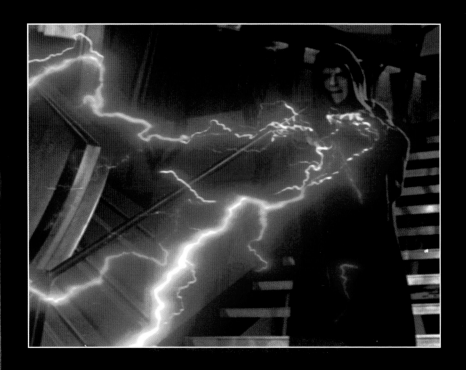

It is time for me to face the
Emperor himself. The Emperor is
very powerful. But at the last
moment, Darth Vader turns away
from the dark side and defeats the
Emperor. The Rebels have won
and the galaxy is free at last.

Glossary

Blueprints
Plans showing a map of where everything is on board.

Daring
Brave and adventurous.

the Force
The special power that both Jedi and Sith can learn to use.

Imperial Academy
This is where the Galactic Empire trains its army.

Jawa
The people who live on Tatooine.

Remote
A long way from anywhere else.

Shield generator
The machine that makes the protective shield around the Death Star.

Sith Lord
A high-ranking member of the Sith race.

Tractor Beam
A beam that can trace other ships and pull them in.

Triumphant
Happy, victorious, jubilant. Usually when you have won something, you would feel triumphant.

Wookiee
A hairy being that lives on the planet Kashyyyk.